CHRISTMAS PLANNER

THIS PLANNER BELONGS TO:

_____

YEAR

OCTOBER

SUNDAY	MONDAY	TUESDAY	WEDNESDAY

THURSDAY	FRIDAY	SATURDAY

NOTES

NOVEMBER

SUNDAY	MONDAY	TUESDAY	WEDNESDAY

THURSDAY	FRIDAY	SATURDAY

N O T E S

_____
_____
_____
_____
_____
_____
_____
_____
_____
_____
_____
_____
_____
_____
_____
_____
_____
_____
_____
_____
_____
_____
_____
_____
_____

DECEMBER

SUNDAY	MONDAY	TUESDAY	WEDNESDAY

THURSDAY	FRIDAY	SATURDAY

NOTES

DECEMBER

1

2

3

4

5

6

DECEMBER

7

8

9

10

11

12

DECEMBER

13

14

15

16

17

18

DECEMBER

19

20

21

22

23

24

DECEMBER

25

26

27

28

29

30

31

ULTIMATE CHRISTMAS
TO-DO LIST

- [ ] _____
- [ ] _____
- [ ] _____
- [ ] _____
- [ ] _____
- [ ] _____
- [ ] _____
- [ ] _____
- [ ] _____
- [ ] _____
- [ ] _____
- [ ] _____
- [ ] _____
- [ ] _____
- [ ] _____

ULTIMATE CHRISTMAS
TO-DO LIST

- [ ] _____
- [ ] _____
- [ ] _____
- [ ] _____
- [ ] _____
- [ ] _____
- [ ] _____
- [ ] _____
- [ ] _____
- [ ] _____
- [ ] _____
- [ ] _____
- [ ] _____
- [ ] _____
- [ ] _____

ULTIMATE CHRISTMAS
TO-DO LIST

- [ ] _____
- [ ] _____
- [ ] _____
- [ ] _____
- [ ] _____
- [ ] _____
- [ ] _____
- [ ] _____
- [ ] _____
- [ ] _____
- [ ] _____
- [ ] _____
- [ ] _____
- [ ] _____
- [ ] _____

RANDOM GIFT IDEAS

RANDOM GIFT IDEAS

RANDOM GIFT IDEAS

CHRISTMAS TRADITIONS

PEOPLE TO SEE

PLACES TO GO

OUTFITS TO WEAR

MOVIES TO WATCH

SONGS TO LISTEN TO

CHRISTMAS WISH LIST

HOLIDAY CARDS TRACKER

NAME		SENT		RECEIVED	

HOLIDAY CARDS TRACKER

NAME		SENT		RECEIVED	

HOLIDAY CARDS TRACKER

NAME		SENT		RECEIVED	

CHRISTMAS GIFT LIST

NAME	GIFT	PRICE	BOUGHT?	WRAPPED?

CHRISTMAS GIFT LIST

NAME	GIFT	PRICE	BOUGHT?	WRAPPED?

CHRISTMAS GIFT LIST

NAME	GIFT	PRICE	BOUGHT?	WRAPPED?

CHRISTMAS GIFT LIST

NAME	GIFT	PRICE	BOUGHT?	WRAPPED?

WEBSITES & STORES

CHRISTMAS
SHOPPING LIST

- [ ] _____
- [ ] _____
- [ ] _____
- [ ] _____
- [ ] _____
- [ ] _____
- [ ] _____
- [ ] _____
- [ ] _____
- [ ] _____
- [ ] _____
- [ ] _____
- [ ] _____
- [ ] _____
- [ ] _____

CHRISTMAS
SHOPPING LIST

☐ _____

☐ _____

☐ _____

☐ _____

☐ _____

☐ _____

☐ _____

☐ _____

☐ _____

☐ _____

☐ _____

☐ _____

☐ _____

☐ _____

☐ _____

CHRISTMAS
SHOPPING LIST

- ☐ _____
- ☐ _____
- ☐ _____
- ☐ _____
- ☐ _____
- ☐ _____
- ☐ _____
- ☐ _____
- ☐ _____
- ☐ _____
- ☐ _____
- ☐ _____
- ☐ _____
- ☐ _____
- ☐ _____

CHRISTMAS
SHOPPING LIST

- [ ] _____
- [ ] _____
- [ ] _____
- [ ] _____
- [ ] _____
- [ ] _____
- [ ] _____
- [ ] _____
- [ ] _____
- [ ] _____
- [ ] _____
- [ ] _____
- [ ] _____
- [ ] _____
- [ ] _____

BLACK FRIDAY PLANNER

SCHEDULE

BUDGET

WEBSITES

STORES

ITEMS TO FIND

NOTES

CYBER MONDAY PLANNER

SCHEDULE

BUDGET

WEBSITES

STORES

ITEMS TO FIND

NOTES

ONLINE ORDERS TRACKER

DATE	ONLINE STORE	ITEM	RECEIVED?

CHRISTMAS ACTIVITIES IDEAS

CHRISTMAS PARTY

DETAILS

THEME

GAMES

FOOD

DRINKS

NOTES

GUESTS

SUPPLIES

DECORATIONS INVENTORY

ITEM	LOCATION	QTY

NEW DECOR & ORNAMENTS TO BUY

DECORATING PLANNER

CHRISTMAS TREE

LIVING ROOM

OTHER ROOMS

CHRISTMAS TABLE

OUTSIDE / GARDEN

NOTES

CHRISTMAS MENU

APPETIZERS

MAIN COURSE

SIDE DISHES

DESSERTS

BEVERAGES

KIDS MENU

GROCERY LIST

RECIPE

PREP TIME :   COOK TIME :   TOTAL TIME :

INGREDIENTS

DIRECTIONS

RECIPE

PREP TIME :   COOK TIME :   TOTAL TIME :

INGREDIENTS

DIRECTIONS

RECIPE

PREP TIME :   COOK TIME :   TOTAL TIME :

INGREDIENTS

DIRECTIONS

RECIPE

PREP TIME :   COOK TIME :   TOTAL TIME :

INGREDIENTS

DIRECTIONS

CHRISTMAS BUDGET

CATEGORY	BUDGETED	ACTUAL

CHRISTMAS EVE

MORNING PLANS

AFTERNOON PLANS

EVENING PLANS

LAST MINUTE NOTES

CHRISTMAS DAY

6 AM

7 AM

8 AM

9 AM

10 AM

11 AM

12 PM

1 PM

2 PM

3 PM

4 PM

5 PM

6 PM

7 PM

8 PM

9 PM

10 PM

THINGS TO REMEMBER

NOTES FOR NEXT YEAR

NOTES FOR NEXT YEAR

Made in United States
Troutdale, OR
11/26/2024

25275190R00044